# Stress Less

*Transforming Stress into Success*

*To Denise
To Your Success*

Copyright © 2014 by Nan E. Martin

All rights reserved. Except as permitted under the U.S. Copyright Act of 1976, no part of this publication may be reproduced, distributed, or transmitted in any form by any means, or stored in a database or retrieval system, without the prior written permission of this publisher.

The information provided in this book is designed to provide helpful information on the subjects discussed. The author and publisher are not offering it as legal, accounting, or other professional services advice. While best efforts have been used in preparing this book, the author and publisher make no representations or warranties of any kind and assume no liabilities of any kind with respect to the accuracy or completeness of the contents and specifically disclaim any implied warranties of merchantability or fitness of use for a particular purpose. Although the author and publisher have made every effort to ensure that the information in this book was correct at press time, neither the author nor the publisher shall be held liable or responsible to any person or entity with respect to any loss or incidental or consequential damages caused, or alleged to have been caused, directly or indirectly, by the information or programs contained herein.

Published by: Experience Life Productions

Printed in the United States of America
First Edition: January 2015

Library of Congress Cataloging-in-Publication Data
Martin, Nan E.
      Stress Less: Transforming Stress to Success / Nan E. Martin

ISBN: 978-0-9909909-2-5

Cover design by Imagine Enterprises, LLC

# Book Testimonials

Nan has done it again with Stress Less. This book is concise, powerful and gives you simple tools to help you eliminate stress easily and effortlessly. The ERASE Formula really works!

                              B. Rasor, Emotional Intuitive

Nan is one of the most gifted and talented coaches I have ever met and worked with. She is on that cutting edge of insight for getting people to a place that they need and want to be. I am so much further along in my life than I ever imagined possible. I owe her a great debt for giving me my life back that I will never be able to pay. With Nan's help, I am now FREE to be and become the person I was born to be.

                                                Jan Pedigo

Nans intuitive guidance and coaching promotes positive change in her clients' lives; and you won't be disappointed with the results. It never ceases to amaze me what limiting beliefs and emotional baggage she can uncover and eliminate for good.

K. Jamison

http://www.experience-essential-oils.com/courage-to-pursue-my-dreams.html

http://www.experience-essential-oils.com/my-life-changed.html

# Dedication

This book is dedicated to each of you who are seeking and wanting to transform stress, or anything else in your life, into *success*.

I believe in all of you!

# Acknowledgements

To my greatest teacher, my Mother, who definitely was far from the perfect Mom or role model, but showed me what not to do and gave me clarity on what not to become. Turning out to be an "opposite" isn't always a bad thing.

To my brother Schuyler Martin for enduring what no man or woman should ever have to endure in one life time. Thankfully we didn't have to walk through it alone, now or then.

To my animals, who have been my best friends, my saviors and my inspiration behind so much that I have done and continue to do.

To my greatest friend and mentor, Barbara Rasor, who has always supported me and believed in my coaching and intuitive abilities long before I could.

To all my AK-DC chiropractor gurus including Dr. Troy Gustafson, Dr. Owen, Dr. Kevin Usry and many others who educated me and put me back together when I was a stressed mess.

To my guardian angels and guides, and my divine creator, for keeping me alive, teaching me, inspiring me, and giving me the courage to bring what I do to the world so I can help others.

To my mentors that are spread far and wide, and are in books and websites, stages and shows, thank you for being the inspiration behind transforming stress to success.

To my love of my life who right now is just me, my spirit and my soul—the girl who never ceases to amaze me, who can walk through fire, who never quits, who can shed skins and transform herself, and inspire others to do the same.

To my clients who continue to inspire me and push me beyond what I know so I can help them transform anything in their lives to a more successful result, and live the life they were born to live.

# Contents

Book Testimonial ............................................................ III

Dedication .................................................................... V

Acknowledgements ...................................................... VII

Introduction – Born to be Stressed? ............................... XI

Chapter 1: Stressed Out and Burned Out America ......... 1

Chapter 2: The Good, the Bad and the Ugly of Stress ..... 5

Chapter 3: The Expression of Stress:
The Mental, Emotional, Spiritual and
Physical Aspects of Stress ............................ 13

Chapter 4: Sending out an SOS – Sources of Stress ...... 17

Chapter 5: The Seven Sinful Stressors .......................... 27

Chapter 6: Triggers, Tigers and Bears Oh My! .............. 29

Chapter 7: The Stress Affect - Physical Body
Systems Affected by Stress .......................... 33

Chapter 8: Three Mistakes to Avoid if Wanting
to Stress Less ............................................... 41

Chapter 9: Transforming Stress into Success
with the ERASE Formula ............................ 47

Chapter 10: Environment ................................................ 49

Chapter 11: Rejuvenation ................................................ 53

Chapter 12: Awareness ................................................... 57

Chapter 13: Strategy – Creating a Strategy
 for Success ................................................... 59

Chapter 14: Equip and Explore ....................................... 61

Chapter 15: Sh*t Happens so Stop Stressing It! ............ 71

Online Resources ............................................................ 73

Appendix ......................................................................... 75

References ....................................................................... 79

About the Author ............................................................ 81

# Introduction
## Born to be Stressed?

From the moment I was conceived I was *stressed*. You may ask "How do I know that?"

I know based on my history. You see, my mother was an asthmatic so she was not only taking medication while she was pregnant but was also drinking and taking other pharmaceuticals. Since a baby is a product of the mother's environment, I was *born* stressed.

But it didn't stop there. My mother was physically and emotionally abusive to me, my brother and even my father. Living in that kind of environment, puts you in *"fight or flight"* mode which significantly stresses the body, particularly the endocrine and immune systems. It also creates perpetual emotional and mental stress as you are constantly *"on guard"* from feeling unsafe and worried about being attacked. Spiritually, I was stressed because I frequently questioned not only *why* this was happening, but *how* there could be such a cruel God that would allow such brutality to continue without anyone noticing or caring about my wellbeing.

My saving grace throughout childhood was the companionship I experienced with my animals. Thankfully, my mother allowed us to have animals despite her allergies and respiratory challenges as long as they *lived outside*. From the day I was born I had an intuitive connection to animals, particularly horses that I couldn't explain or understand.

At age 5, my mother gave into my persistent and nagging requests to allow me to learn how to ride, and thankfully she signed me up for riding lessons and horse camp in the summer. By age 7, riding was surviving; it was the only thing that helped me get through to the next ride. For my mother it was a convenient excuse for why I was hurting, bruised, and beat up, so she supported my equestrian enthusiasm as it helped justify her actions.

Riding and competing on a national level in the hunter-jumper discipline taught me responsibility, focus and hard work which I loved; and provided tools for me to be successful in school, college and later in Corporate America. I learned to thrive under stress, pressure and negativity. I clearly understood and was living the famous quote – "That which does not kill us makes us stronger" ---*Friedrich Nietzsche*

But…..I was still missing something….

By my third management job in Corporate as an Environmental Consultant, I got very good at dealing with stress, but not letting go of it! This proved later to be almost *fatal* as my body continued to accumulate stress on all levels: emotionally, spiritually, mentally and physically.

By 35, I was burnt out, stressed out and living on the mental edge trying to find the harmony between my work and personal life. I had chronic fatigue and multiple health challenges and was emotionally shut down due to so much unresolved trauma from my past.

When I hit bottom and got fired from my corporate job it wasn't pretty but I realized that I couldn't live my life how I was living it. I had to find a way to start releasing the stress and the buried emotional trauma from the past to move forward in a new way.

From that point forward, I began to research and try almost every known stress busting method there was available. I worked with multiple people in the healing arts to recover my mental, emotional and physical health.

Thousands of hours and dollars later, I finally figured out what to avoid and what tools to use to live my life in harmony with the world and environment around me. One of the key shifts I made was understanding that I needed to make better choices for myself every day no matter how uncomfortable they were; and to *commit* to those choices. It was the only way to change and to *live*.

I wrote *Stress Less* to help everyone out there trying to find some sense of peace and freedom from the stresses of life. My intent is that this simple and easy to read book and the ERASE Formula will not only help you understand the good, bad and the *ugly* of stress but make you aware that you can change it, if you choose to!

Here's to choosing *Less Stress* in all of our lives at work and at play! An exercise a day keeps stress away!

# Chapter 1
## Stressed Out and Burned Out America

Most people encounter stress everyday but don't understand what stress is, what triggers it or even how it affects our mind and body. As a matter of fact, so many people are *numbed out* by stress that they aren't even aware that it is their new normal! Yikes!

Now before you start beating yourself up or panicking because you just realized I was talking about YOU, understand that most of us were really not taught how to release stress, and we certainly were not given the tools to do so. This is especially true in the United States were education and culture itself is so focused on *doing* rather than *being*.

As a matter of fact, most of us were taught to stuff and hide stress along with our *emotions* which can be a deadly combination. How we *respond* to stress depends on how we were taught to handle it and our family's belief systems towards stress. Those who don't stuff stress away, often times become addicted to it without even being aware that they are hooked into it on an emotional level. There is a another group of people that like to use stress as a reason to complain and stay in their personal excuse story; or use it to control what they can't control.

Most people can't be placed strictly in one group, but I was clearly in the *addiction* category. I loved the endorphin/adrenalin rush which I will explain later; and honestly it seemed like the *trendy* thing to do. The person the most *stressed* was the winner! The winner of what is the question!

## Questions to Consider?

- What is my family's version of stress?
- How do I respond to stress?
- How was I taught to respond to stress?
- How do my children respond to stress?

## The Proof is in the Statistics

Just in case you needed some more proof to demonstrate how stressed all of us really are, here are some *alarming* statistics:

- According to the Center for Disease Control, 80% of visits to the doctor are believed to be related to stress! Really? Then why are we not addressing the root of the stress?

- According to the Everest College's Annual Work Stress Survey, 83% of Americans are stressed out by at least one thing related to work. In 2012, this number was 73%! In one year, this number went up by 10%! This is a disturbing upward trend that we are not even aware of.

- Gallup-Healthways Well-Being Index found that at least 45% of entrepreneurs experienced stress "*yesterday*". Didn't we quit our corporate jobs so we could stress less?

- According to the American Psychological Association, Stress in America Survey 2013, 36% of Americans say their stress has increased over last year and 42% say their stress has increased over the past five years. They also report that 38% of adults overeat or eat unhealthy foods due to *stress*. The most frightening statistic was that the teenage stress numbers were within 1% mark of the adult numbers! We are passing on our *poor stress habits* to our children and bringing up a generation of stressed people that also do not know how to cope, release and free themselves of stress.

Yup, its official and the proof is in the Stats! *WE the PEOPLE of AMERICA have officially become stressed out and burnt out beyond recognition!*

We, as Americans, understand the *benefits of stress relief* but we are not taking action to change and we are passing it on to our children and raising generations of stressed out families.

Still need more evidence? The proof is in the pudding or the picture in this case! Search online for photos of President Obama in 2008 and 2014; and compare the photographs. He has more grey hair, more wrinkles and just looks exhausted. The stress of the office has certainly taken its toll on our President and many other Presidents that have come before him.

And it's taking toll on you, your family, your work or business and even your pet. It's undeniable the effects of stress…

*It's time to learn how to do stress differently. If you can't commit to change for yourself, do it for your children or for your family or your pet!*

# Chapter 2
## The Good, the Bad and the *Ugly* of Stress

If you want to resolve or change something that isn't working for you, you must understand what it is, why you are doing it and why it is important to change it. Otherwise, you won't change because you won't have an understanding on what needs to be done or how to go about it.

So therefore, if you want to *stress less*, then first you must know what stress is and how it is defined. According to Mariam-Webster's Dictionary *stress* is defined as:

**A constraining force or influence: as ---**

*a*: a force exerted when one body or body part presses on, pulls on, pushes against, or tends to compress or twist another body or body part; *especially* : the intensity of this mutual force commonly expressed in pounds per square inch

*b*: the deformation caused in a body by such a force

*c*: a physical, chemical, or emotional factor that causes bodily or mental tension and may be a factor in disease causation

*d*: a state resulting from a stress; ***especially*** : one of bodily or mental tension resulting from factors that tend to **alter an existent equilibrium. ie, job-related** *stress*

*e*: strain, pressure. Example: the environment is under *stress* to the ***point of collapse*** — Joseph Shoben

In simpler *Nanglish*:

***Stress is the body's response* to *stimuli which can be positive (good) or negative (bad) that is triggered through various Sources of Stress (SOS).***

When you are triggered and it's infrequent it's all good! When you are triggered by one or more SOS and it is a daily occurrence, then it starts to get *bad*. When you don't change and it becomes a routine, it gets *UGLY*!

**What is Good Stress?**

Good stress keeps you excited about life and motivates you to take action in a positive way. It can even boost immunity and give you energy! The technical term for you techies and science buffs is *eustress*.

Some examples of GOOD stress are:

- Fight or Flight Response – when used to preserve or save life only! The body is designed to create and release hormones to be able to respond to a life threatening or dangerous situation *automatically*. When this happens you will breath faster, your pulse and heart rate will quicken and you will have more energy! Short term this is required to save your life! And this is good!

- Exercise - When used as a positive outlet it can boost immunity, support healthy function of your heart and cardiovascular system and even improve mood by releasing stress.

- Excitement – Getting excited! Going to an amusement park and riding your favorite big coaster! Or starting something new or going to an event. Or even competing in a race or team sport.

**Questions to Consider?**

- What good stress do I have in my life?

- If you don't have any good stress, what could you do to create it?

**When Good Stress goes *Bad*. And Bad Stress turns *Ugly***

When things that create good stress are overdone and/or you start to become triggered by one or more SOS on a daily basis, good stress can go *bad*.

There is a universal law, called the *Universal Law of Polarity* or LOP, that illustrates why and how this can happen. Universal Laws or *Laws of Nature* are unchanging principles that govern how our world and the universe itself can exist and create.

The LOP states that there are always two sides to every situation, emotion or problem. The easiest way to explain this is in terms of *opposites*- two extremes of the same thing. This is why anything in *moderation* generally supports us and anything overdone generally does not: When you live on the extreme ends of anything it will create an *imbalance*.

If you continue to live imbalanced or on one end of the spectrum eventually it becomes *bad* and most of the time turns *ugly* as your body is not meant to continually exist in the *extremes*. This is why when we do, often times we will experience a wakeup call or an AHA moment that creates the awareness we need to change.

**Questions to Consider?**

- Do I need a wakeup call?

- Am I living on the extreme edge in one or more areas of my life?

- Did I already have a wakeup call, but I didn't recognize it as such?

Imagine a Seesaw. Being on a seesaw with a friend creates a positive stress since you can enjoy the moment, laugh and tell jokes and take turns going back and forth. This is how the Seesaw maintains balance or equilibrium.

However imagine being on that same seesaw by yourself. Good stress would start to turn bad real quickly, since there is no one on the other side to create the *equilibrium*. You are now stuck until you find a friend or figure out how to counter balance the other extreme.

My point here is…..

***In life you need to create the harmony between the two extremes to maintain your sanity and to stress less. It is your resond-sibility and your choice—no one will do it for you. You also cannot do it for others---they are either willing to play or they are not!***

In terms of stress, when we experience good stress it can support us mentally, emotionally, spiritually and physically. But when overdone, it can turn bad as the body is not designed by the Law of Polarity to maintain that state.

**Warning Levels and Signs of Imbalances due to Stress**

The body has a loving and caring "*built in warning mechanism*" that gently cautions you and warns you that you are in a place where you need to re-establish your equilibrium before it gets bad or ugly. Recognize that they can be emotional, physical or mental.

Here are some signs:

- **Mental** – Forgetfulness, worrying about everything, losing the ability to concentrate and focus and constant negative mind chatter.

- **Emotional** - Feelings that you are overwhelmed or losing control; increased emotional vulnerability such as anger and irritation, or sadness and hopelessness.

- **Physical** – Fatigue, headache, stiff and tense muscles, sleeplessness, suppressed immunity making the body more vulnerable to colds and infection.

These are generally some of the first signs that our body and mind is challenged by stress and that the systems are starting to "break down" on some level. So this is Warning Level 1 that something is not working and needs to change.

But...

When the warning signs are continually ignored, and our physical and emotional health starts to deteriorate (Warning Level 2) then the bad stress can turn *ugly*! When the stress is ugly, you have hit bottom (Warning Level 3) and are grounded out on the seesaw until something changes!

**Questions to Consider?**

- Am I ignoring the warning signs?
- Am I at Warning Level 1, 2 or 3?
- Am I afraid to change?
- What level do I have to hit before I am willing to change?

**From Good to the Ugly Scenario**

I want to give you an example of how stress can go from good to ugly so you really get this-this is so important! Exercise is a perfect one to use, since it is almost always viewed as good.

Here is how exercise which is a tool for relieving stress and promoting a healthy body and mind can turn ugly.

- **Good** – Exercise slightly stresses the physical body which may create slight muscle soreness. But because exercise helps to release stress and produces *"feel good"* hormones when you exercise called *endorphins* it is good. Yay! Good!

- **Bad** – You exercise way too much to the point where the body can't recover so the benefits of exercise are *outweighed* by the body's inability to repair tissue and regain energy. Your muscles are overexerted and you are on the brink of becoming chronically fatigued. This is not so good….

- **The Ugly** – You exercise out of a need to create an adrenalin rush and/or *endorphin* high (explained later). And it starts to replace an emotional or mental void, or an unresolved issue in your life. You are literally running from and avoiding the thing that you need to see the most by replacing it with something else (substitution). Exercise is now *feeding* the stress and has become an *ugly* habit! This person is literally *living* at the gym, they are freaking out when they can't get there or if the gym is closed on a holiday!

I was very good at the *ugly.* In my twenties I ran 20 miles plus per week, rode my horse three or more times per week, worked out in between in addition to working my 50+ hour a week job as an Environmental Consultant. And at one time I even attended Manhattan College during the evenings to get my Master's Degree in Environmental Engineering! Believe it or not, if there was any time left, I would hit the bar!

That life style got me very sick and tired with chronic fatigue. And then it got *ugly*. On one of my trips to the Caribbean to unwind (lol), I got intestinal parasites. By the time, I realized what I had and found a person that knew what I was experiencing and how to treat it, I could barely eat or get out of bed.

But then, the ugly incident turned promising when….

I realized I needed to not only find ways to release stress but to address all my unresolved childhood issues that I was running from else it was even going to get *uglier*. And for a while it did; but when I was willing to change and take responsibility for ME, my actions, my words and my wellbeing and my life everything started to transform from ugly back to bad. And then when I transformed to good, I began to unleash the real success in my life and find the harmony that I was looking for!

**Questions to Consider?**

- Am I taking a stress reliever from good to bad?

- Am I taking a stress reliever from bad to ugly?

- Am I afraid to change?

- What level do I have to hit before I am willing to change?

# Chapter 3
## The Expression of Stress: The Mental, Emotional, Spiritual and Physical Aspects of Stress

Last chapter you learned about the good, bad and the ugly of stress.

*But how is stress expressed?*

*Stress is expressed through the mental, emotional, spiritual and physical aspects of self that are mostly programmed in your body and mind from experiences and belief systems acquired during childhood. Researchers have shown that by the age of eight, 80% of our beliefs have been formed. Belief systems determine how we think and, more importantly, how our sub-conscious responds to everything in our life including stress. So, we need a new and improved strategy to fix it.*

This is where our society really misses the boat. Even when we see the two sides of the coin we don't always see the details. One of the reasons people are not *transforming stress into success* is that everyone is so focused on the *physical* side of the problem!

This is very interesting to me, since we are the *physical representation* or *manifestation* of our mental, emotional and spiritual parts. Together they make up who we are, what we belief and how we respond to things.

So to be successful at erasing stress we need to consider and address all the parts and the sum of the parts!: And the programming *that we were taught as children that is subconsciously telling us how to respond to stress.*

**Life isn't just about the physical: We need to include it into our strategy for success along with the other components but not make it the only part we address. We are a spiritual being with cognitive function (mental) having an emotional experience in a physical world!**

I like to view people as a four pointed star where the points are the Mental, Emotional, Spiritual, and Physical (MESP) aspects of self; and the center of the star is where your unique and authentic self and soul lives and plays.

Your star lives in an environment where it is surrounded by a loving and caring divine source and creator from which you were born. From here you can connect, love and express life and live to your greatest potential if you allow it. You can get everything you need and want if you allow it.

The sum of the MESP aspects and how they synergistically work together which also includes how you live, your beliefs, your values, etc. dictates how bright your star will shine in this world. Stress not only dims the light but creates haze around the points so you can't get a sense of direction. It literally blocks *everything* – your dreams, your visions, your hopes; and your true purpose and potential.

So….

In order to have less stress and become that shiny star, we must address all four aspects of the expression of stress; and make adjustments and change as necessary. There is no such thing as a one sided star—all the points are there even if you can't see them.

You are buried somewhere under all that stress and the emotional and mental baggage that comes with it. I can see that the stress is not who you are--can you?

**Questions to Consider**

- Am I willing to look at all the aspects of self to be and to live stress free?

- Am I willing to make adjustments to become a shining star? And turn stress into success?

- Do I want to become a shining star? And live my life with purpose?

- Who took that star?

**PS Each one of you was born and is a shining star. Don't let anyone take that from you, including yourself.**

# Chapter 4
## Sending out an SOS – Sources of Stress

Sources of stress can be mental, emotional, spiritual and physical as we learned from the last chapter. To better understand what is triggering stress, we must know where it is coming from.

Mental and emotional stress leads to physical stress, so let's start there.

**Mental and Emotional Stress**

Mental and emotional stress lead to *physical* stress. While mental and emotional stresses are very different by definition, they are difficult to separate out since technically emotions have a *mental* aspect.

However with that said, there are sources of stress that undoubtedly have emotional and mental roots; and ones that clearly have one aspect over the other. How you view this is based on your belief system and experiences therefore it may not be apparent to everyone.

Some of the most common mental sources of stress are:

- Studying for exams or tests
- Overcommitting or overbooking self personally and professionally
- Work related deadlines
- Negative talk/Mind chatter
- Questioning self
- Computer work

Some of the most common emotional stressors are:

- Divorce or breakup of relationship
- Family emergencies
- Death in the family

As you see, mental and emotional stressors can and do clearly overlap, but the examples used above contain more of one component than the other.

Then, there are some sources of stress that have both emotional and mental roots. These are:

- Moving
- Change of job, profession or career
- Retirement
- Illness, injuries or surgery

- Financial loss

**Questions to Consider**

- What is your largest source of emotional stress?
- What is your largest source of mental stress?
- What SOS has both components?

**Sources of Spiritual Stress**

Many may dispute this point and see there is no such thing as spiritual stress; and that is OK. My intent in presenting this section and even writing this book is to open your awareness to what you are currently or not currently *experiencing.* The only way you can do that is by getting out of your comfort zone and being open to different ways of thinking and being.

I honor everyone's choice to believe in a higher power and creator, or not; it is not my place to judge that or change that. As a matter of fact, I think that it is very important to honor how you do choose to honor that part of you, not how everyone else would choose it for you. That alone will create stress as you are not honoring yourself, your wishes and your inner part of you, your spirit and soul.

Spirituality when viewed from this angle is about that connection with yourself that so many of you have lost. It is that connection that gives you direction, brings you hope, follows your dreams, inspires you; and really knows who you are and what you bring to the table in this life time. I lost it-it was buried under all my childhood BS to the point where I couldn't function. I was sick, tired, frustrated, angry and lost. Well that was certainly stressful! Sound familiar to anyone?

Which leads me to the concept of spiritual stress....

What I just touched on was spiritual stress. My spirit, my soul, my divine creator and all the universal forces were trying to show me different. But I was so shut down mentally, emotionally and spiritually, I didn't get it. But eventually I did—I was open to changing and found the right tools to transform stress into success!

You see...

I believe that everything happens for a reason. When you don't see it in the moment it is because your perception of the situation which is based on your belief systems, doesn't allow you to see any differently. And your mind including what you were taught gets in your way. Your subconscious mind was designed to keep you where you are and stopping you from seeing what needs to be changed. This is emotional, mental and *spiritual* stress.

To me this is our spirit and our divine creator, trying to move you a certain direction or to help you see things differently. And sometimes it does, but we don't recognize it until we are down the road a bit. Right?

How many times have you looked back on something whether you got sick, the car broke down or you got fired from your job, and said that "it was a blessing in disguise" or "that saved my life". All of the big, small and "tragic" events in my life were blessings. They showed me that whatever I was doing wasn't working or how my family responded to situations wasn't the best way for me to do it. And I learned different ways to let go and walk through *anything*. And now I can help my clients do the same.

When we are in the middle of "the event" it is the most stressful thing in our life! These periods of transition are stressful-mentally, emotionally, spiritually and physically. But there is a way to walk through it if you choose to do so.

***Once again stress is an ongoing reminder that the MESP parts of us or mind, body and soul cannot be separated out and they must be in harmony for us to live the life we want to live. Call IT what you want, but call yourself out on IT if you want to follow and pursue your dreams.***

## Questions to Consider

- What event(s) changed your life completely?

- What AHA moments did you have from those events?

- What events that didn't turn out so well, are you holding over your head?

- What is spirit showing you and teaching you about stress?

## Sources of Physical Stress

Physical stress is the category that most of us can relate to. And it is the one we give the most thought to, although by now you have learned that we need to address stress from all aspects not just the *physical*.

Here are some of the top physical sources of stress:

- **Environmental Stress**

- **Illness and Injury**

- **Sleeplessness**

- **Poor Nutrition/Diet**

**Environmental Stress**

In today's world we are exposed to more toxins in the environment than ever before. Our bodies tolerate it very well but we were not designed to combat and accumulate toxins on this level. This completely overtaxes our system and stresses the body therefore it is very important to also release the toxicity—else we become the new hazardous waste sites of the 21st century. I know I used to clean them up, and then I was one.

With that said, environmental stress includes the following:

- Toxins from our food, pharmaceuticals and over the counter drugs

- Chemical and heavy metal toxins, radiation, pollution, etc. from the outdoor environment

- Electromagnetic pollution from lights, power lines, computers, cell phones, etc.

- Herbicides and pesticides

- Chemical household cleaners and personal care products

The more you expose your body to in terms of toxins and chemicals, the more stress your body will be under. Your body has to process and cleanse toxins from the body else they are stored until it can find a way to release it. Reducing the toxic load on the body will allow your body to better cope with stress.

Use natural personal care products and clean with green products in your home that are non-toxic to your children, pets and the environment.

**Illness and Injury**

This is a double edged sword. Chronic stress can create illness, as noted by the AHP and once your body is in that state it contributes to more stress. Chronic illness and/or injuries, including pain, can not only be a physical source of stress but also an emotional and mental source of stress. Dis-ease creates dis-harmony and stresses all the body systems until equilibrium is restored.

For people battling chronic illness in particular it is so important to have and follow a *stress less* strategy. In an article published by *BMJ Supportive and Palliative Care*, it was found that massage therapy had a positive influence on the stress levels of those suffering from serious illnesses. And that massage could help to release emotional and physical stress even in late stage diseases.

My Mom was in the hospital many times in her life, especially the last years of her life. I found them to be very stressful places in general. There have been huge improvements over the years, but way more can be done (and the same goes for the work place environment). I was surprised that when my Mom's breast cancer came back and was progressing, how little support she was given on the stress side of things. She was given no tools to help her emotionally or mentally process her distress or dis-*ease*.

Tools such as meditation, essential oils and massage can be incorporated into the daily programs. My Mom always asked for oils and used them religiously to help her relax, Especially sacred frankincense from Young Living Essential Oils. In the end it was one of few tools she had left to help her relax, let go and transition; and she was thankful for it despite the disapproval of most of her doctors.

Incorporate a strategy to erase stress into your life and don't let people take it from you.

**Sleeplessness**

Stress is notorious for disturbing sleep patterns and affecting our quality of sleep. We all experience occasional sleeplessness and that is normal. However when sleepless nights becomes the norm then it gets *bad*. And when stress gets to the point that we are chronically not sleeping as in staring at the ceiling all night and waking up multiple times throughout the night with a racing mind it becomes *ugly*.

The National Heart, Lung and Blood Institute recommends the following amount of sleep per age group:

- **Children at School Age**: 10 hours

- **Teenagers**: 9-10 hours

- **Adults**: 7-8 hours of sleep

Sleep plays a very important role in reducing stress on a mental, emotional, and physical level as our body and brain needs time for rest and recovery. Lack of sleep affects our mental concentration, focus, mood and can creates high blood pressure and a host of other health issues.

When you don't get enough sleep, your ability to handle stress significantly drops off. According to the American Psychological Association, Stress in America Survey 2013:

- 45% of adults report feeling more stressed when they have less than 8 hours of sleep

- Those adults report symptoms of stress such as irritability or anger (45%), feeling overwhelmed (40%) and lack of interest (42%)

Also, 35% of teens report that stress caused them to stare at the ceiling wide awake at night over the course of a month. And those teens sleeping less than eight hours per night experienced a 42% increase in stress!

Ok people, time to get some sleep so we can transform stress into success!

**Diet/Nutrition**

Studies have shown that some drinks and food can magnify stress and decrease our ability to cope and release stress. Once again, it doesn't mean avoid them all together (LOP), but it does mean that in times of high stress that eating the right foods is a strategy for success.

The top five foods and drinks that can exacerbate or trigger stress are:

- Processed or fast foods with high "bad" fat content

- Coffee, tea and hot chocolate
- Soda, soft drinks and energy drinks
- Sugar and candy
- Alcohol

Stress is known for depleting vital nutrients, minerals, enzymes and antioxidants which the body needs to function properly. While the food we eat can supply some nutritional value, most health professionals agree that it is just not enough even when we are not stressed!

I am always amazed at how many people don't take a good whole food source multivitamin, antioxidant and probiotic daily especially people who are under a lot of stress which seems like everyone these days. I also take enzymes and Omega-3 Fatty Acids with Vitamin D daily; and supplements and essential oils to support the healthy function of my endocrine and immune systems.

For success you always have to be creating and building a good foundation and this includes nutrition. If you want to transform stress into success, make sure you are supporting your body nutritionally as well.

## Questions to Consider

- I am drinking or eating certain foods in excess?
- Am I supporting my body with core foundational nutrition?
- Is there one drink or food item that I can live without?

# Chapter 5
## The Seven Sinful Stressors

According to the American Psychological Association, American Institute of Stress in New York, here are the seven top causes of stress.

- Job/Work Pressure

- Financial Concerns

- Health and Wellbeing

- Relationships

- Poor Nutrition/Diet

- Media Overload

- Sleep Deprivation

The scary part of this list is that most of my clients I speak with initially are experiencing four or five out of seven sinful stressors! Just one of the stressors can throw a person out of balance!

These causes speak for themselves and I have addressed most of them head on in other parts of the book. The point here is to see that most of us are experiencing one or more of the seven sinful stressors!

**Questions to Consider**

- What is my top stressor from this list?
- What stressor could I change immediately?
- What is stopping you from making that change?

# Chapter 6

## Triggers, Tigers and Bears Oh My!

So far we have talked about what stress is and how it can turn from bad to ugly, the sources of stress, and even how it is expressed.

In this chapter, you will learn what a trigger is and how the body *automatically* takes over!

**Fight or Flight Response of the Nervous System**

Out magnificent body is designed with a built in *automatic* mechanism called *Fight or Flight*. Its purpose is to create and release chemicals and hormones to be able to respond to a life threatening or dangerous situation *automatically*. This is how we can *react* quickly to a situation without *thinking* about it.

What triggers the Fight or Flight system can be different for everyone, but in general it is dependent on your perception of a threat which may be real or perceived. For instance, if a tiger or bear is approaching you, the system will be *triggered* as that is a real threat!

Triggers can be anything you see, smell, hear, taste or feel as they are perceived through our senses. They are also influenced by your belief systems or experiences from childhood.

For instance, if I had a negative experience at my Grandfathers home as a child, my body may perceive that home as a *threat*. The brain will create a memory around the event based on what colors, smells, sounds, etc. were present that day, how I felt emotionally (scared or angry) and your belief system. The memory is stored in the limbic system of the brain—our center of emotion.

If I experience that combination of stimuli again, either in part or in whole, or I am in a similar situation, the memory is *triggered*. And then the Fight or Flight response will take over automatically.

This is why negative emotional and traumatic experiences not only affect your health but also create tremendous stress when they go resolved. The interesting thing is that sometimes the triggers are so subtle and may be brought on by something so insignificant as a simple conversation with your boss or coworker, that you don't recognize them.

**Questions to Consider**

- Do I know what is triggering my stress?

- Am I willing to look at and understand my triggers?

## The Automated Message

When the Fight or Flight system is *triggered*, hormones such as cortisol and adrenalin (epinephrine) are created and pumped into the bloodstream. Your pulse and heart rate will speed up, your breath will become rapid, and your muscles may become tenser in preparation for you to take action on the *threat*.

Short term (acute) triggering of this system is a good thing -- it is meant to *save* your life! This is how you or an animal can act immediately to run from a predator!

But here's the problem….

If the system is *chronically* stimulated and overworked, the life preserving hormones start to *suppress* the body's functions that they originally supported! And continue release of these hormones changes your body chemistry from alkaline to *acidic.* When that happens, it starts getting *ugly*.

*Remember the Law of Polarity from Chapter 3?* This is another example!

# Chapter 7
## The Stress Affect - Physical Body Systems Affected by Stress

Stress can blow out your nervous system and is the main system that is affected by stress; however, all of the physical body systems are secondarily affected by *stress*. That is the *stress affect*.

As a matter of fact, according to the *American Psychological Association*, it's the effect on the other systems that is a problem, not necessarily the nervous system itself:

***"Chronic stress, experiencing stressors over a prolonged period of time, can result in a long-term drain on the body. As the sympathetic nervous system continues to trigger physical reactions, it causes a wear-and-tear on the body. It's not so much what chronic stress does to the nervous system, but what continuous activation of the nervous system does to other bodily systems that become problematic."***

And this is why things can turn from bad to *ugly!* The physical body systems that are affected by stress include:

- Nervous System

- Cardiovascular
- Musculoskeletal
- Respiratory
- Endocrine
- Digestive
- Immune
- Reproductive

A brief description of the physical body systems and the corresponding affect are presented below.

**Nervous System** - consists of the spinal cord, brain, sensory organs, and all of the nerves that connect and communicate these organs with the rest of the body. This system is responsible for the *Fight or Flight* mechanism.

**Cardiovascular System** – is comprised of the heart, blood vessels, and the blood. According to the *American Psychological Association (APA), "Chronic stress, or a constant stress experienced over a prolonged period of time, can contribute to long term problems for heart and blood vessels. The consistent and ongoing increase in heart rate, and the elevated levels of stress hormones and of blood pressure, can take a toll on the body. This long-term ongoing stress can increase the risk for hypertension, heart attack or stroke."*

**Musculoskeletal System** – Headaches are one of the most commonly reported complaints associated with stress.

The APA states *"Muscle tension is almost a reflex reaction to stress — the body's way of guarding against injury and pain. Chronic term stress causes the muscles in the body to be in a more or less constant state of guardedness. When muscles are taut and tense for long periods of time, this may trigger other reactions of the body and even promote stress-related disorders. For example, both tension-type headache and migraine headache are associated with chronic muscle tension in the area of the shoulders, neck and head"*

**Respiratory System** – The respiratory system emotionally is connected with releasing since we let go through the breath. It is so common for people to hold their breath when stressed! And it is the one thing that can really help people release it quickly.

*The APA* explains further, *"Stress can make you breathe harder. That's not a problem for most people, but for those with asthma or a lung disease such as emphysema, getting the oxygen you need to breathe easier can be difficult."* They add that this may trigger an asthma attack or panic attack. Once this happens now a person needs to manage a physical and an *emotional* trigger.

**Endocrine System** – The endocrine system consists of glands which secrete hormones that regulate the activity of cells or organs. They travel through the circulatory system to where they are needed; and act as chemical messengers so the body can respond *instantly*.

The pineal, pituitary, pancreas, ovaries, testes, parathyroid, thyroid, adrenals and hypothalamus are the major glands. The pancreas and digestive system also has a role in the hormone production; and are therefore affected also.

When the body begins to stress, the hypothalamus sends a signal to the autonomic nervous system and the pituitary gland to create cortisol and adrenalin (epinephrine) or *"stress hormones."* The adrenal glands produce these chemicals which supports the *Fight or Flight Mechanism*!

This eventually may lead to adrenal dysfunction or fatigue or what is referred to as "General Adaptation Syndrome" or GAS and termed by Hans Selye. He describes this stage as Exhaustion Stage as the body is now depleted of energy and can no longer adapt to the stressors.

But wait there's more….

When stress hormones are released and we are in *Fight or Flight*, our liver produces more blood sugars in the form of glucose so we have the ENERGY to take ACTION.

The *APA* states *"For most of you, if you don't use all of that extra energy, the body is able to reabsorb the blood sugar, even if you're stressed again and again. But for some people — especially people vulnerable to Type 2 diabetes — that extra blood sugar can mean diabetes. Who's vulnerable? The obese and races more inclined to diabetes, such as Native Americans."* Wow! One more reason to release the stress! This also stresses the pancreas, since the pancreas as an endocrine function, is responsible for regulating blood sugar levels.

**Reproductive Systems -** The male and female reproductive systems which are associated with the endocrine system are severely affected by stress as more and more hormones are released into the body. Cortisol which supports healthy functioning of the circulatory, cardiovascular and reproductive systems in excess can create weight gain, imbalance and other associated issues.

For men, according to *APA*, *"ongoing stress over an extended period of time, can affect testosterone production, sperm production and maturation, and even cause erectile dysfunction or impotence."*

For women, stress may affect our menstrual cycles, menopause, sexual desire and mood associated with hormonal cycles. The APA further explains *"premenstrual symptoms worse or more difficult to cope with and pre-menses symptoms may be stressful for many women. These symptoms include cramping, fluid retention and bloating, negative mood (feeling irritable and "blue") and mood swings."*

*Release the stress to improve your mood, sex life and attitude!*

**Immune System -** The immune system is a complex system of cells, tissues, and organs that synergistically work together to not only protect the body from infection but to fight it. It is body's natural defense system. Once again short term stress can support this system and may even boost immunity, but long term stress compromises the system.

In *Psychological Stress and the Human Immune System: A Meta-Analytic Study of 30 Years of Inquiry*, Suzanne Segerstrom and Gregory Miller determine:

*"The results of this meta-analysis support this assertion in one sense: Stressors with the temporal parameters of the fight-or-flight situations faced by humans' evolutionary ancestors elicited potentially beneficial changes in the immune system. The more a stressor deviated from those parameters by becoming more chronic, however, the more components of the immune system were affected in a potentially detrimental way."*

Have a goal to improve your overall wellness? Reduce the stress to support your immune system

**Digestive System** - Stress has been contributed to digestive upsets, heartburn, excessive stomach acid, ulcers and more. The interesting part is that even the medical researchers confess that there is an emotional and mental component beyond the *physical* that they can't completely understand!

According to the Harvard Mental Health Newsletter, August 2010:

*"Functional gastrointestinal disorders affect 35% to 70% of people at some point in life, women more often than men. These disorders have no apparent physical cause — such as infection or cancer — yet result in pain, bloating, and other discomfort."* Furthermore, *Multiple factors — biological, psychological, and social — contribute to the development of a functional gastrointestinal disorder and stress can trigger and worsen gastrointestinal pain and other symptoms, and vice versa."*

Emotionally and mentally the digestive system is tied in with assimilating and processing what is bothering or "eating you". This is why when you are *emotionally* upset one of the first things that may be affected is your *stomach*. The colon or large intestine (and the lungs) are also associated with *letting go*, so if you are not allowing yourself to breath and let go it may manifest as *constipation*.

I constantly had an upset stomach when I was a child as I was always trying to process why my mother was so angry and upset most of the time. I had to learn how to "stomach it" because I didn't know how to process it. Once we can assimilate or understand mentally and emotionally why something is happening then we can let it go and breathe it out!

**How Does This Help Me Transform Stress?**

Understanding how your body works and the affect stress has on it, will help you recognize and be *aware* of what is happening to your body.

***Your body's ability to response to stress is compromised on all levels once the nervous system is triggered. Each day you are either doing things to support and create more longevity and vitality in your life or extinguishing it. What are you choosing? And if you are not choosing to support yourself, your body and your mind-Why Not?***

**Questions to Consider**

- What physical symptoms do I have that I now can contribute to stress?

- What system(s) in my body is showing the greatest sign of stress?

- Are you supporting life and longevity?

# Chapter 8
## Three Mistakes to Avoid if Wanting to Stress Less

There are many mistakes to avoid if you want to *stress less* but here are the top three. They are:

1. Overcommitting Self
2. Living in the Past or Future
3. Negative Self Talk

**Mistake Number One: Overcommitting – Winning the Superhero Contest**

These days we seem to be in a superhero contest called *"Who can jam more in one day than anyone else!"*

This is because many of us as children were taught more is more, not more is *less*. We were taught to measure ourselves based on how much we could get done, what was completed or crossed off our list, rather than accomplishing what was important for the day; and what got us closer to our goals. And if we didn't complete the list, we were told we were not good enough, couldn't cut it, or we were doing something wrong.

So we run around like a chicken with our head cut off, stressed to the max beating ourselves up emotionally, spiritually, physically and mentally. This is pretty bad, and in the long run it turns *ugly*.

Everyone needs to give themselves permission to just say NO and without the ADD-ONs. Add-ons are the reason and justification why we CANT say NO. We learned them because we didn't want to offend anyone, hurt anyone's feelings, let anyone down or be RUDE.

Let go of what is not serving you, taking from your time and energy and stressing you out. This includes people, things, meetings, organizations, clubs and clutter.

**RUDE AWAKENING No. 1** – You can and need to take care of your own needs first. Retire the Superhero outfit so you can stress less and get comfortable with saying NO.

## Mistake Number Two: Living in the Past or the Future – Not Living NOW

So many people live in the past or in the future and not in the present moment. This creates mental and emotional stress that manifests as physical stress.

You cannot change your past by focusing on what was; what you could have done or should have done; or by beating yourself up or everyone else up about it!

The way you change what happened in the past is by changing your attitude or response to the events in the moment. Try this very easy technique to release the past (or please don't if you would like to remain stuck).

**ACCEPT** where you are AT NOW. Yes, you have to ---you don't have to like it, but you do have to accept it. Stop blaming everyone and take accountability for YOUR part even if your part is just a pin prick. Otherwise you will be a VICTIM of your circumstances forever. (Remember the LOP).

**FORGIVE** yourself and the people who taught you, screwed you or screwed with you! Let go of the spite, anger, resentment, grudges, disappointment, and self-pity party.

Now I recognize that some of you were brutalized, beat up and victimized; and experienced more Drama-Trauma than *Dalai Lama*, and I respect that because I was THERE. So in those cases, it may take a lot more work than running through this exercise a few times, but it's a START!

And…lastly….

**RELEASE IT!** And do it each time you find your subconscious mind dragging you down *Self Sabotage Lane*! You won't regret it.

Living in the future creates a similar stressful result but the trigger is FEAR. Fear you can't do it, fear there won't be enough, fear you aren't enough, fear something will happen to you or someone else, etc. You become so fearful and you get so far ahead of yourself that you begin to literally have "*an out of body experience*".

You know you have had them. I've had them, we all have had them. At first, you can't feel your feet and you may feel like you're going to faint and you definitely can't concentrate. And then your body starts to panic because you are NOT PRESENT. Your mind is in the future somewherein fear and your body is here. This stresses the body on all levels!

**RUDE AWAKENING No. 2** – You manifest or create your future by how you think and what you emotionally *embody* in the present. If you are stressed, you are creating more STRESS! Come back to Earth; face your skeletons in the closet and your fears so you can *stress less* and create the life you want!

## Mistake Number Three: Negative Self Talk – Mind Chatter

Our subconscious mind is designed to keep us stuck in patterning and belief systems that no longer work for us. That part of us loves to replay the negative tapes, remember the disapproving voices of our past and create destructive mind chatter.

The constant negative mind chatter creates a huge amount of mental, emotional and physical stress that wears us down, keeps us up at night and holds us back from believing in ourselves.

When this occurs you need to take control of your mind. I like to say to my body, STOP, as a child I may have not had a choice but as an adult I do. I have a CHOICE right now in this moment to STOP beating myself up and I do.

**RUDE AWAKENING No. 3** –You can choose to STOP the negative self talk and tapes. Stop beating yourself up and start to be mindful of how you are treating yourself today. Begin to be kind and loving to yourself so you can *stress less* and love yourself more today!

# Chapter 9

## Transforming Stress into Success with the ERASE Formula

To be successful at anything in life you need to have the right *environment*; a *rejuvenated* mind and body; an *awareness* of what needs to change; a *strategy* or plan to follow; and the correct *equipment* or tools to accomplish the task.

Imagine building a home without choosing the landscape first; or trying to build a home when you are on the brink of exhaustion; or using plans from the 1920's; or having the incorrect raw materials.

*Would you be able to build the house successfully?*

The answer is obviously no, because the house would not have the proper planning or foundation to be a success.

Releasing Stress is no different. To transform s*tress into success* you need to incorporate all the correct elements into your daily routine so that your mind and body is built from a solid foundation; and you aren't heading down *Self-Sabotage Lane*. The ERASE Formula does just that – builds a foundation and maintains it. Use it to release stress or create a successful foundation for any project in your life.

# Chapter 10
## Environment

The first part of the ERASE Formula is Environment. This includes your inside environment and your outside environment.

**Supporting Your Internal Environment**

Here are the top tips to support your internal environment:

- Eat healthy and nutritious foods

- Don't forget to take your vitamins

- Exercise or take a walk

- Breath – don't hold your breath

- Let go of the negative self talk

- Get out in nature

To support our internal environment we must provide the nutrition and fuel for our body to cope with stress more efficiently. Eating healthy and nutritious foods, taking your vitamins and drinking water are three of the simplest tools we can use to *stress less*. Foods with high vitamin and mineral levels such as fresh fruits and vegetables, whole grains and fish, help to reduce stress levels and make us feel better mentally and emotionally.

We must also BREATHE. Breathing initiates the body's natural relaxation response. It is one of the best free tools we have to help us relax and let go of stress yet it is the one we use the least. Want less stress? Stop holding your breath and laugh way more! More to follow in the tools section.

Exercise has such great benefits on all levels. We all know about them so I won't explain here. If you can't get out to the gym and don't have a lot of time, walk a few minutes a day; shovel a little snow; sweep the porch. And make it fun! It not only kicks in the feel good hormones but helps us to breath.

Finally let go of negative self talk! It not only stresses you out mentally and emotionally, but it drains your energy and doesn't support your growth. Refer to the chapter on three things to avoid for more tips and an exercise to help you STOP this.

**Supporting Your Outside Environment**

We have to maintain the harmony between our outside and inside environments to be stress free (POS). Here are some things to consider:

- Create a sacred space for yourself

- Bring the outside in with flowers, plants and essential oils

- Don't allow negative people be your environment

Creating a sacred space for your self can not only be relaxing but rewarding. It's important to have a space that is just for you whether it is at your office or at home (or both) to reduce stress. Part of why we get stressed is that we are out of our own surroundings – so bring it to you! Take the time to put up pictures of things that not only relax you but excite you!

And change it around as you change. Remove the photos that don't represent where you are going and who you want to be. Throw away the clutter so you can think straight. And consider removing or putting things away that stress you.

Lastly, don't allow toxic people to bring you down to their level and intoxicate your environment. Don't hang out with Debbie Downer – you are not obligated to do so even if they are your family! If you want to be an Eagle than fly like one; and hang out with other Eagles--sorry turkeys.

**Stress Less Action Items**

- Create a space that supports the life you want to live

- Take a break and spend some time enjoying the outdoors

- Diffuse some essential oils in your home, office, barn or clinic

# Chapter 11
## Rejuvenation

Rejuvenation is the next part of the ERASE Formula. Our body, mind and soul needs time to rejuvenate.

Rejuvenation includes:

- Getting enough rest and sleep

- Scheduling reflection and quiet time for self

**Rest, More Rest and Sleep**

As discussed in Chapter 4, the National Heart, Lung and Blood Institute recommends eight hours sleep to ensure that your body has enough time to repair at a cellular level, to refresh the body and mind; and to cope with stress. Anything less puts you in a state of deprivation and increases your stress level.

To ensure you are getting adequate sleep and good quality rest, sleep away from lights and noises in particular. Even pulling televisions out of your bedroom can help. New studies have shown that LED lights and blue lights in particular can decrease your melatonin or sleep inducing hormones. Blue light will actually keep you up at night!

Use alarm clocks and other methods that are less disruptive of your sleep cycle such as the Philips Wake-up Light. Use essential oils to help you wind down before bed and relax so you can *stress less*.

**Reflection Time**

Scheduling quiet time for yourself is a wonderful way to reconnect with our inner self and discover parts of you that can be hard to find in the hustle of everyday life. Creating "you" time, teaches you how to stay in the present moment and start to embody a state of *being* rather than a state of doing.

Most people have a hard time enjoying time with self as quiet reflective time was mostly associated with negative behavior especially when we are children. We were placed in "time outs", sent to our rooms to contemplate our bad behavior or placed in "detention" and not allowed to speak. I rarely interpreted reflective time as a good thing till later in life; and then it seemed brutal just sitting and doing nothing for more than ten seconds!

I had to retrain myself to be comfortable just being with me and my thoughts. But once you do, you will really love this time for yourself! Take a walk, soak in a bath with some essential oils or find someplace that is quiet and just breathe and let go.

**Stress Less Action Items**

- Go to sleep earlier

- Throw away the LED lights and alarm clocks; and get an alarm clock that won't disturb your sleep cycle

- Use essential oils, meditation and relaxing music to help you get a better night's sleep

- Schedule quiet time for self at least once per week preferably at least 5 minutes per day.

# Chapter 12
## Awareness

If you want to transform stress in your life to success, you must have an awareness of when you are becoming stressed, what is causing you to get stressed (triggers) and the reasons why you are choosing stress in your life (root cause of stress/belief systems).

Most people are not even aware that they are *stressed* as they are so used to living in that state that it becomes their new norm!

Finding the *triggers* that create stress can be a bit tricky since we tend to protect ourselves from seeing them especially if resulting from childhood or adult traumas or negative experiences. In this case it may be safer for you to stay stuck then being aware of the pattern that can set you free.

I have my client's keep a very small notebook with them at all times to keep track when they are triggered or when they start to feel the first signs of stress. I have them write down everything about the environment: what time it was, who was there, what was being said, what they saw, smelled or heard; and anything else relevant.

Keeping a log has several benefits. First you may see a pattern that you are not aware of when you review your entries. Second, you create a record since when you are triggered often times we forget the details of what is happening. Third, you become a loving observer of yourself in a non-critical and non-judgmental way.

Lastly, consider taking a yoga or meditation class. This will help you to become more comfortable with being still, quiet and centered, which in turn will increaseyour *awareness.*

**Stress Less Action Items**

- Buy a small notebook for purse or briefcase to keep track of triggers

- Be aware of negative self talk and mind chatter. And stop it

- Sign up for a yoga or meditation class

- Practice being a loving observer of self

# Chapter 13
## Strategy – Creating a Strategy for Success

To release stress successfully we must have a plan; and commit to following the plan or make changes to the plan as necessary.

A sure way to fail at anything that is important to you in your life is to have no plan. Operating on this level is like being on a ship without a destination.

Instead of choosing where you want to be and how you will get there, you allow the wind, the weather and the tides to dictate where you will be. That actually creates mental, emotional, spiritual and physical stress because you are not supporting yourself or your success. When you don't have a direction and don't ask for help in finding it, you are not allowing the Universe or your Divine Creator to show up for you and support you on this wonderful journey. As a matter of fact you may be sabotaging it!

Think about it, if you set a course to sail from Florida to Antigua how would you get there without charting a course, having the boat prepared for your trip, having food and water for you and your crew; or having tools on board to support your journey or to correct a problem.

While it is essential to stick to a plan and see it through, it is also important to remain flexible to allow for course corrections due to weather, wind direction, or unforeseen challenges.

Your strategy to transform stress into success is to use the ERASE formula. So many people have goals to be healthier, lose weight, feel better, and live longer; and to grow spiritually, professionally and personally. If we make *stressing less* our top priority than the other goals will be easier to achieve!

**Stress Less Action Items**

- Create a strategy to stress less.

- Choose at least one action item from each ERASEcategory to incorporate into your schedule for 30 days then add another one. If you have fully embodied what you have learned and are successful at it, then you may move along quicker. If you haven't then stay the course until you have!

- Print out and place the ERASE Formula somewhere where you can see it to remind yourself each day to stay the course.

# Chapter 14
Equip and Explore

The last part of our ERASE Formula is Equip. We must equip ourselves with the best tools for the job. The challenge is that most of us have not been given the tools to release stress or the triggers that *create* stress.

Imagine building a home without a set up plans or even a measuring tape or hammer. It would be very difficult to even get the plot laid out correctly so you could begin to build the house. You need the right tools to stress less and build success!

In the United States and many other modern cultures, people are taught to *do* and not to be. We were rarely taught relaxation methods as children which means that we need to teach ourselves now. We need to find tools and techniques to lower our stress and teach our body that it is OK to relax and let go!

The good news is there are so many fantastic tools that you can use; some of which have a minor learning curve and others such as breathing that are free!

The real work is in the commitment to working the plan. Sorry Charlie, No Commitment-No Success. The hammer can't build the house without you, the ship can't sail to the destination without you and stress won't magically disappear without some work.

As with all tools, its best to explore and experiment to find the ones that truly resonate and help you, else you won't use them; and your plan here is to transform stress into success, right? What works for your friend may not work for you—and that's OK! Make sure you try at least one tool per day to keep stress away!

Here are the top tools for releasing stress:

- Breathing
- Essential Oils
- Animals
- Laugh and Play
- Meditation
- Music
- Massage
- Releasing Triggers/Transforming Belief Systems

**Breathing**

When people are stressed they tend to hold their breath and forget to breathe! It is the easiest and best way to breathing. Breathing is the easiest and best way to initiate the body's *natural relaxation response*. This "Relaxation Response" was first discovered and coined by the American Institute of Stress Founding Trustee Dr. Herbert Benson.

When the response is activated, your body goes to a deep rest where the emotional and physical responses to stress are minimized. You will find your breathing becomes slower along with your heart beat; your blood pressure lowers and even your muscles relax. Isn't that amazing?

For best results, AIS recommends practicing deep breathing 20-30 minutes a day. But, here's a thought—let's start with 3! Breathe in deep and count to 3, then hold it for 3, then breathe out for 6; and then *repeat.* Get in the habit of doing this first, and then increase your time when it becomes easy!

Another technique is combining breathing with a smell. Use a flower, a plant or better, an essential oil. Smell the oil while breathing for even better results!

**Essential Oils**

Essential oils are one of nature's best kept secrets and are one of my favorite tools for releasing stress. They are not only very easy to use but can be easily taken with you anywhere.

Oils are very different than herbs and are obtained from properly distilling the volatile liquid of any part of the part including the seeds, roots, bark, stems, leaves, fruit, flowers or branches.

Oils are very powerful stress releasers as your nose is the only sense organ that is hard wired to your brain; and more specifically the part of the brain that controls our emotional responses called the amygdala.

The amygdala is considered the "center of emotions" and not only stores the emotional memory and triggers to stress, but initiates in part the Flight or Fight response which was presented earlier, remember that?

This means with the whiff of an oil, and the amygdala as well as other limbic parts of the brain can be influenced instantly!

For instance, Lavender is considered an adaptogen. Adaptogens help the body adapt to imbalance or specially stress! Not all oils are adaptogens, but most oils can not only assist us with our ability to handle stress but any emotion that is associated with stress such as irritation, anger or distress.

Oils can also help to balance the mental, emotional, spiritual and physical aspects of stress that I discussed earlier in the book. In my experience and studies of natural remedies for stress, essential oils are one of the only tools, besides my coaching techniques, that can provide support on all these levels.

There are many different grades of essential oils, but I recommend and prefer to use therapeutic grade oils due to their purity, frequency and ability to change patterning in the body very quickly. Please note that most of the oils found in cosmetics and personal care products are fragrant grade oils and are called "adulterated" by the industry since many contain synthetic materials. These oils due to their impurity and adulteration will therefore not have the same effect on the body and mind; and may even in some cases be harmful to the body rather than supportive, so please do your research when selecting oils.

The oils I use from Young Living Essential Oils not only can be used topically, but many can also be taken internally as a dietary supplement. Using oils in this way can also support the body in releasing stress.

Please refer to my website, Experience-Essential-Oils.com to learn more about essential oils and how to use them. Two of my favorite oils to support me in releasing stress everyday are Stress Away and Joy essential oil blends.

**Animals**

There's nothing like having a pet in the home to ease stress after a hard day. As a matter of fact, studies are mounting on the enormous health benefits that animals provide for people especially with regards to lowering stress related health risks such as high blood pressure and stress hormones such as cortisol.

As a matter of fact in the article, *Animal-assisted therapy — Magic or Medicine?* Written by JS Odenaal, people had a decrease in blood pressure and therefore other physiological effects within 5 minutes of positive dog interaction! Wow and cortisol levels also decreased significantly.

One of the most interesting studies I found regarding pets and stress was conducted on a group of New York City stockbrokers which were hypertensive (high blood pressure). In the study *Pet Dog or Cat Controls Blood Pressure Better than ACE Inhibitor* by the University at Buffalo showed that the stockbrokers who were already receiving an ACE inhibitor and also received a pet were able to significantly lower blood pressure and heart rates over those that didn't receive a pet as part of the study.

Dr. Karen Allen, Ph.D., stated *"This study shows that if you have high blood pressure, a pet is very good for you when you're under stress"*. She also showed in a previous study that blood pressure and heart rates were reduced when participants were in the presence of an animal and performing tasks designed to provoke mental and physical stress.

For those of you who own animals, a study isn't needed to confirm that you *stress less* around the company of your animals; but it is sure nice to have the study to back what you knew all along. I knew- as a child and teenager, my animals were one of the only things that helped me experience what it was like to be stress free. My animals were one of the only things that kept me going and believing as a child and teenager.

And today they continue to be part of my support system. Their endless unconditional love, never-ending energy and enthusiasm for life is just the kind of tool we all need and want. I *stress less* everyday thanks to my animals.

If you don't have an animal, often times you can volunteer at a local animal shelter or non-profit organization that works with or has animals for adoption. If you do this, work at several until you find the one that resonates with you! That way it will be part of your success strategy to stress less rather than just adding one more thing to your list.

**Laugh and Play**

So many of us have forgotten to laugh and play as adults. Laughing and playing allows stress to melt away quicker than anything.

I take breaks with my dog Dezie in between clients. We walk, throw the Frisbee and just shake off whatever the day is bringing. I am always pleasantly surprised (awareness) how just taking a few minutes to walk outside (environment and strategy) to laugh and play rejuvenates my mind (rejuvenation) and body so I'm ready to go back to work.

Don't you so appreciate how animals teach you and inspire you to just be in the moment, and love, laugh and play?

Whatever inspires you to laugh and play, take the time to do it for a few minutes each day to stress less. It helps you to breathe, let go and experience more love and joy every day!

**Meditation**

For thousands of years, cultures have used meditation for mental, emotional, spiritual and physical wellbeing. In modern societies, studies have confirmed what ancient cultures already knew which was that meditation not only prevents stress from affecting the body, but helps to eliminate the effects of stress that are cumulative.

My favorite form of meditation is Transcendental Meditation or TM which I learned over 25 years ago. I recommend exploring your options and go with something that works for you. A recent study found that Transcendental Meditation helped college students increase coping ability and decrease psychological distress (stress) including lowering blood pressure and more.

Wow! Can you imagine how learning some of these tools in school would have helped us to eliminate stress as an adult?

The biggest challenge with meditation can be in learning it, especially in today's society where we have a hard time stopping our mind chatter which reduces your ability to focus and stress less.

The good news is that there is a technology called binaural beats that will override much of the mind's ability to focus. Brainwave entrainment technology puts your brain into the same state as when you are meditating! And has the same benefits.

There are great resources for this technology including the Monroe Institute which is a nonprofit education and research organization specifically focused on the exploration of human consciousness. They have various recordings and CDs that will help you focus and release stress very quickly! Personally, I'm a big fan of the Hemi-Sync CDs so check it out and see if it is the right tool for you!

## Music

We know music can change our mood instantly but can it help with stress? The short answer is YES! Since music has an instant effect on your emotional state it can relax your mind, your muscles and even your stress hormonal level, particularly cortisol.

This primarily occurs as researchers at Stanford University (press release 2006) have said by changing brain waves that are similar to those that occur in sleep. Their findings found that music makes an easy stress reduction tool. Studies have also found that slow and/or classical music has the most benefits when it comes to slowing pulse and heart rate, lowering blood pressure and decreasing stress hormones.

So this one is a no brainer! Put on your music in your car, in your bath and in your home and office; and allow stress to melt away.

**Massage**

*BMJ Supportive and Palliative Care* shows that massage therapy can help. The study indicated that massage therapy had a positive influence on the stress levels of people suffering serious illnesses such as brain cancer.

Researchers suggest that massage therapy can improve the emotional and physical well-being of patients with late stage diseases. When used in combination with standard care, massage therapy can help reduce stress, anxiety, pain and fatigue and increase quality of life.

And with this established, synergize your massage by using combining them with other stress busting tools such as aromatherapy or deep breathing exercises!

**Releasing Triggers/Transforming Belief Systems**

If you are still having a hard time relaxing and letting go of stress despite using the tools that are provided here it is time to get serious about those triggers, tigers and bears. More than likely when you get stuck here your body and mind are responding to triggers, emotions and beliefs that are deeply rooted in either childhood or a traumatic event; and you probably need some help seeing your way through.

I understand this as my body was hard wired in this way and I thought I would never be able to change it. The good news is that you can with some help. One of the first books I read that opened my eyes to this was *Feelings Buried*

*Alive Never Die* by Karol K. Truman. Reading that was like turning on a light; and became some of the foundation for my work I do today.

That was another one of those AHA moments that was a blessing in disguise. There were many more of them that followed thankfully and I carry less stress today than ever before.

You can do it to---I believe in you….

**Stress Less Action Items**

- Choose at least one action item from each ERASE category to incorporate into your schedule for 30 days then add another one. If you have fully embodied what you have learned and are successful at it, then you may move along quicker. If you haven't then stay the course until you have!

- Explore all the tools until you find the one that works best for you.

- Combine one or two tools and create your own stress less success strategy!

- If the stress less tools are helping but not releasing the triggers to stress then consider coaching to transform stress to success.

# Chapter 15
## Sh*t Happens so Stop Stressing It!

The only thing you can change in your life is YOU or more specifically your *response*. You cannot change people or stop things from happening. There are going to be days that it appears that the world is falling apart: the kids wake up puking; the dog ate something and you have no idea what and are rushing to the vet; or the car won't start and it's the one week your neighbors are on vacation and you have no transportation or help!

SH*T HAPPENS!

But you do have the power to change how you *respond* to stress---it is your *respond-sibility*! Blaming others or the situations that create stress does not resolve it but digs us in deeper to being a victim of our circumstances. I know that you hate that word and the thought of that—and that's good! I hope that it will help you see it for what it is. So you can...

Learn to walk through it....

And see the hidden message and the reason behind it before you judge it, beat yourself up for it or run away from it.

As it could be your blessing in disguise, your AHA moment when you choice to...

***Transform Stress into Success!***

Here is to your Success! And the life you want to live, enjoy and explore!

Make the *choice* to experience stress free living today!

***With Love and Appreciation***

***Nan***

# Online Resources

**Stress**

- Experience Stress Free Living: Nan's website for stress advice tips and Bonus Chapter. www.ExperienceStressFreeLiving.com

- Experience Essential Oils: Nan's website for learning about and purchasing therapeutic grade essential oils. www.Experience-Essential-Oils.com

- The American Institute of Stress: www.stress.org

- The American Psychological Association: www.apa.org

- National Institute of Mental Health: www.nimh.nih.gov

**Essential Oils**

- Experience Essential Oils: Nan's website for learning about and purchasing therapeutic grade essential oils. www.Experience-Essential-Oils.com

**Music/Meditation**

- Monroe Institute www.monroeinstitute.org
- Transcendental meditation www.tm.org

**Massage**

- American Massage Therapy Association: www.amtamassage.org
- National Association of Massage Therapists www.namtonline.com

*Print out or copy the next page, and place the ERASE Formula somewhere where you can see it to remind yourself each day to stay the course.*

## Stress Less
*Transforming Stress into Success*
## with the ERASE Formula

**E-nvironment: Breathe, Eat Right, Exercise, Create Sacred Space**

**R-ejuvenation: Rest, Reflect and Renew**

**A-wareness: Loving Observation of Self and Triggers to Stress**

**S-trategy: Committing and Working a Plan to Stress Less**

**E-quip: Using and Exploring tools such as Essential Oils, Meditation, and Music to Transform Stress to Success. And taking time to Play with your Kids and Pet!**

*Nan E. Martin*
*Your Personal Executive Coach*
*ExperienceStressFreeLiving.com*

## Stress Less – Transforming Stress to Success Bonus Chapter

Thank you for purchasing Stress Less – Transforming Stress to Success! As a special gift to my readers, I am excited to present a special bonus chapter just for you! This will help you get clear on your ERASE Strategy for Success.

Please go to

www.ExperienceStressFreeLiving.com/bonus-chapter.html

and claim your bonus chapter today!

In Service and Gratitude

Nan

# References

Allen, Karen, Ph.D., University at Buffalo, The State University of New York, "Pet Dog or Cat Controls Blood Pressure Better than ACE Inhibitor" Nov 1999.

American Psychological Association. Stressed in America. January 2012 and 2013.

Everest Report by Harris Interactive , 2013 Work Stress Survey, March 2013

Friedmann, E.; Son H. "The human-companion animal bond: how humans benefit" *Vet Clin North America Small Animal Practice* 2009 Mar; 39(2): 293-326.

Gallup-Healthways Well-Being Index, Entrepreneurship Comes with Stress but also Optimism, December 2012

Grimshaw, Heather. "A Four-Legged Cure." *Thrive*. July 2008. (May 4, 2009)

Harvard Health Publications, Harvard Mental Health Letter, "Stress and The Sensitive Gut", August 2010

Harvard Health Publications, Harvard Medical School. "Pets and your health." *Harvard Men's Health Watch*. June 2008.

Mariam-Webster's Dictionary

Nidich SI, Rainforth MV, Haaga DAF, et al. A randomized controlled trial on effects of the Transcendental Meditation program on blood pressure, psychological distress and coping in young adults. *American Journal of Hypertension.* 2009; 22(12):1326–1331.

Odenaal, J.S. "Animal assisted therapy: Magic or medicine?" *Journal of Psychosomatic Research.* Volume 49, Issue 4, 275-280. 2000.

Saling, Julia; Keir, Stephen Thomas "Pilot study of the impact of massage therapy on sources and levels of distress in brain tumour patients" *BMJ Supportive & Palliative Care* (2012)

Segerstrom, Suzanne C.; Miller, Gregory E. "Psychological Stress and the Human Immune System: A Meta-Analytic Study of 30 Years of Inquiry" *Psychological Bulletin*, Vol 130(4), Jul 2004, 601-630.

Suarez K, et al. "Psychological Stress and Self-Reported Functional Gastrointestinal Disorders," *The Journal of Nervous and Mental Disease* (March 2010): Vol. 198, No. 3, pp. 226–29.

Thoma, Myriam V, et al Thoma MV, La Marca R, Brönnimann R, Finkel L, Ehlert U, et al. (2013) "The Effect of Music on the Human Stress Response". PLoS ONE 8(8): e70156. doi:10.1371/journal.pone.0070156

# About the Author

Nan was born into an environment that appeared picture perfect from the outside but it was far from that. Mental, emotional and physical abuse and drama-trauma colored most of her childhood with negativity to the point where she even attempted to take her own life when she was a teenager.

Her animals, particularly her horses, were her source of unconditional love and understanding; and riding became *surviving*. Nan used that encouragement to succeed in the equestrian disciplines of hunters, jumpers and equitation, from the time she was a child and then well into her adult life as a professional trainer and rider.

Despite traumatic childhood experiences, Nan was always determined to overcome anything in front of her. She understood somewhere in her soul that there had to more to life then what was presented to her; and she sought to find it.

After college, Nan worked as an Environmental Scientist and Consultant for some of the top engineering firms. She went back to school to receive a master's degree in Environmental Engineering which led her to managing multi-million dollar Superfund, hazardous waste and health and safety projects for Fortune 100 Companies such as UPS, General Motors and IBM.

Even though Nan climbed the corporate ladder of success and had achieved more than most in her field, she felt like something was still "*missing*" so she continued to work to find the gap. But with this came an enormous price on her health. Nan had several health challenges which she now calls "blessings" as they opened the door to her not only investigating the mind-body connection and alternative health fields but to find a different strategy to release stress and find harmony in her life since what she was doing was clearly not working. It also gave her the courage and *understanding* to face all the unresolved childhood issues that continued to plague her mentally, emotionally, spiritually and physically.

This was a huge turning point in Nan's life as she saw that she was choosing to be the victim of her life and her circumstances rather than manifesting the life she wanted.

From there, Nan left corporate and set out to find the missing piece which translated to a move to Arizona, becoming a personal trainer, opening her own equestrian business and facing yet more health challenges. In 2006, after spending thousands of dollars on self-help programs, books, medical and alternative doctors, healers and gurus and another move to Florida, she found the "piece" she was looking for. This tool allowed her to discover her authentic self and reprogram her subconscious mind that was filled with negative thoughts, unresolved trauma and uncontrollable negative emotions; and finally change the course of her life quickly and dramatically.

Part of Nan's challenge was finding the right mentors that had a style that could support her without negating her history. Nan says *"You have to find that balance, especially when your letting go of the triggers or charged emotions that are programmed in your subconscious mind—you need people on your team that honor where you are at but also hold you accountable to doing the work you need to do personally and professionally so you can and will move forward. That is an art and attribute of an extraordinary coach that is hard to find; I also am able to provide that support to my clients since I've been in those shoes."*

Fortunately, Nan also discovered therapeutic grade essential oils which became and still is one of her best tools for erasing stress and letting go of emotional trauma-drama. She not only built one of the largest free resources for oils on the internet but authored an online training class, *"Using Essential Oils for People and their Animals"* so people could understand how to use the oils safely and wisely; and choose oils using their own intuitive sense.

Nan's intuitive gifts, ability to walk through anything and transform her negative childhood events from stress to success, not only gave her the determination to break through barriers for herself but for her clients around the world. The piece she found is now the core foundational work of her coaching program and is changing lives across the globe.

*"I always heard from people that I needed to stick with one thing-- one career, one home, one goal and just do it. That was never me—I never fit into that box or the "stereotypical life" we all are supposed to live. All I knew in my heart was that life should and could be different and I could make a difference for myself and others if I could find out how to really change it. And I did. Later in life all those childhood traumas, career changes, health challenges and life's bumps in the road led me to my dream career and life that I was looking for. It has made me the "go to coach" for busy executives and entrepreneurs since I have so many life experiences to pull from. I am so blessed!"*

Nan privately works with her client's one on one via phone and in transformational break through intensives to transform anything in life from stress to *success*.

## Connect with Nan Martin

www.ExperienceStressFreeLiving.com

www.Experience-Essential-Oils.com

www.facebook.com/ExperienceStressFreeLiving

www.facebook.com/ExperienceEssentialOils